CW00504446

MY TAKE ON LIFE

Poems by
Jim Smith

Some in the Scottish Dialect

OTHER BOOKS
BY THE SAME AUTHOR

"Tam o'Shanter"
A Translation into English in Verse
ISBN: 978-0-9954971-1-5

TO MURIEL

My long-suffering wife,
without whose encouragement and forbearance
this book, and several of the poems in it,
would never have seen the light of day.

Published in Great Britain in 2015
by Jim Smith

ISBN: 978-0-9954971-0-8

Artworked, printed and bound in Scotland by
Robertson Printers, Forfar

Foreword

I have enjoyed poetry for as long as I can remember. It is a wonderful way to tell a story and I love the discipline of meter and rhyme and the whole rhythm of a well crafted poem.

Where did this love of verse come from? Well, there was always a lot of singing in our house when I was growing up. My father seemed to know every lyric to all the popular songs of the day, and all of my sisters loved to sing too. On top of that, most of our entertainment in those pre-television days was of our own making. I can remember ghost stories being told around the fireside in the evening, and being fascinated by Robert Service's "The Shooting of Dan McGrew" and other exciting poems he wrote about gold, the harsh life, and his adventures in the Yukon.

Encouraged at school, and by my parents, I was entered for the Burns Federation Schools Recitation Competition in 1946 at the age of 11, and won the Will C Cockburn Award for the best performance in competition. The prizes were a much treasured facsimile copy of The Kilmarnock Edition of Robert Burns, a postal order for £5 and a Certificate of Merit for Distinction in Scottish Literature!

I started writing my own poetry as a boy and had a few efforts published in the School Magazine, one of which, 'In Memoriam', is reprinted here. I have also selected just one of my early poems in the Scottish Dialect, 'On the Passing Away of our Budgie'. By the way, it is sheer coincidence that both of these are about death!

During my working life I carried on writing verses whenever it seemed appropriate, like recording special events or by way of thanks. Taken out of context most of them would not be very meaningful to a general audience, so I am only going to inflict two of them on you! One is from my Naval days, 'Thank You for My Farewell Dinner', and the other is about a Speakers Conference held in Sheffield in 1996.

I have never stopped reading and performing poetry and I still enjoy Rudyard Kipling and, of course, Robert Burns. I also much admire Pam Ayres for the seemingly effortless way she can weave a funny story.

Limericks have always been great fun to write. Telling a story in five lines and getting that surprise twist into the ending is really satisfying. Scottish place names can be particularly difficult to rhyme and, because so many of them have three or four or even five syllables, it's not easy to make them fit the rhythm of the limerick. Some years ago I set myself a challenge that whenever I went to speak at a new place, I would write a limerick about it to include in my talk. You will find a few of them in this book.

In the last few years I have been writing poems on much more general themes, particularly on things I feel strongly about and subjects that appeal to my sense of humour. When I have been out speaking to groups, the response to them has invariably been positive and countless people have asked why I have never had them published.

So here I am at the ripe old age of 81 putting together my first book, this wee selection of my poetic efforts, which should give you an insight into my personal take on life.

I hope it will provide plenty of food for thought and, perhaps more importantly, a lot of laughs along the way.

Jim Smith,
2015

CONTENTS

CONTENTS

KIRRIEMUIR

The wee red town of Kirriemuir
Is steeped in history,
There's kirks and wynds and Pictish stones,
And tributes to its famous sons.
So much to do and see.

It doesn't have a cinema
And it's nowhere near the sea,
But there's a pirate ship up on the hill,
Where Peter Pan is living still,
And children all play free.

There are festivals of every sort,
Music, dance and song,
If acting's how you spend your time,
There's 'Opera' and 'Pantomime',
You really can't go wrong.

The townsfolk have inventive ways
Of supporting charity:
'Relay for Life' and swimming 'Splash'
Have raised enormous sums of cash
For them to give away.

So why not come to Kirriemuir
If you haven't been there yet.
See the Gairie glide through the Den of Kirrie,
See a fairy fly at the home of Barrie.
It's a town you won't forget.

THE GARDEN

Oh! I do hate the work of a garden,
Horticulture's not my cup of tea.
It's so much more fun just to lie in the sun,
Or sit in the shade of a tree.
But the march of the weeds is relentless,
With their roots at least one metre long,
While the plants 'cultivated' are all constipated,
And none of them ever look strong.

In the springtime, with best of intentions,
I drag all the tools from the shed.
Then I dig and I hoe and I plant and I sow
Till my fingers are all sore and red.
So I gradually lose my momentum,
And my stints with the spade become few,
Until all my resolve has been known to dissolve,
Leaving more things for Nature to do.

Now I certainly don't have green fingers,
Though I've tried every veg. in the book.
But I need no wheelbarrows to transport my marrows,
And my beetroots are too small to cook.
Then again, in the floral department
I'm singularly short of success:
My attempts at sweet peas just come up to my knees,
And my roses the same, more or less.

Oh! I don't like the work in the summer,
When the grass needs a haircut each week.
Then there's edges to trim and rough bits to strim,
And I don't have my sorrows to seek.
For there's lots of dead-heading and pruning,
And there's weeding to fill up my day,
And more wifely orders, like 'clean out those borders'
And 'make sure it's all tidied away'.

Then the autumn is just a disaster,
Picking up all those leaves is so hard.
When the wind's from the west that's when I like it the best,
For they fall in my neighbour's back yard.
But as my luck would most often have it,
The eastern wind's in my face,
I rake them and stack them, but before I can sack them,
They're blowing all over the place.

Mother Nature's so bent on destroying
All the order I try to create.
Why do miniature shrubs and those dwarf plants in tubs
Grow to six feet, or seven, or eight?
And my neighbours have got such nice gardens,
So neat they beat mine by a mile.
But when winter winds blow, and down comes the snow,
They will all look the same, and I'll smile!

Oh! I do hate the work of a garden,
It's back-breaking, boring and tough.
I've put up with the pain in the cold wind and rain
But now feel I've just had enough.
So I'm going to do something about it
Before I go out of my head:
I will rip out the lot, every plant, bush and pot,
And put in slabs and gravel instead.

OH! THE SNOW

"Oh great! The snow!" The Young Boy yelled,
  "Let's go outside and play.
While school is closed with frozen pipes,
  We'll make snowmen, have snowball fights,
And just have fun all day."

"Oh yes! The snow!" The Student roared,
  "Let's take off for Glenshee.
We'll ski the slopes while there's still light,
  Then party on into the night,
Enjoying the après-ski."

"Oh good! The snow!" The Waterman crowed,
  "That fills me full of cheer.
No matter what the summer brings,
  With snow melt to fill up the springs,
No fear of drought this year."

"Oh well! The snow!" The Roadman said,
  "No sleep for me this night,
I'll drive the 'Gritter' far and near,
  To keep the main roads safe and clear –
And the overtime's alright!"

"Oh dear! The snow!" The Mum exclaimed,
  "Can't let the children skive,
I'll drive them up to the school gate,
  And, hopefully, we won't be late,
I've got the 4-wheel drive."

"Oh damn! The snow!" The Commuter moaned,
 "It really isn't fair,
I'll have to clean off the car again,
 Unless I clear out the garage, and then
Start keeping the car in there."

"Oh hell! The snow!" The Old Man groaned,
 "It just makes me see red.
Clearing the drive is a constant pain,
 And the snowplough just piles it up again!
I think I'll go back to bed."

AUCHTERMUCHTY

A poet was finding it tough tae
Get a rhyme for the toon Auchtermuchty
 When he finally fun' it,
 He threw up his bunnet,
Cryin' "hip hip hooray, it's ma burthday!"

Note: *All Rs pronounced with a Burr*

SORE FEET

I got up one fine morning, but when I tried to walk,
A stabbing pain shot through my heel, my face went white as chalk.
I hobbled through the morning and all throughout that day.
I thought, "If I just move about, this thing will go away".
           I hoped it would.

But nothing seemed to help it, so in a week or two,
I took it to the Doctor, to see what she could do.
She listened to the symptoms, and nodded when I said
It was worst when I'd been sitting down, or just got out of bed.
           So far, so good.

"You've got Plantar Fasciitis", she quickly diagnosed,
"You've stretched the band of tissue that joins your heel and toes.
Your ankle's rolling inwards, we call it 'over-pronation',
It causes lots of tiny tears and painful inflammation".
           How very shrewd.

"It's not a new phenomenon, it's been around for years,
In the British Army Infantry it drove strong men to tears.
When workers all wore tackety boots, the threat was very real.
In the days of 'Bobbies' on the beat it was called 'Policeman's Heel'!"
           That made me brood.

"There's no simple way to fix it or make it go away,
But you could try gentle exercise to stretch it every day.
And wear stout shoes with inserts for increased arch support,
And cut back on the walking, and no energetic sport".
           As if I could!

I asked how long all this would take, for I had plans to make,
Her answer was equivocal, she gave her head a shake,
"Just follow my advice" she said, "right down to the letter,
Take two pain killers when it's sore, and keep it till it's better!"
I understood.

So I stuffed my shoes with insoles and cushions for my heels,
'Twas like walking in stilettos, you girls know how that feels.
My muscles ache, my joints are sore, it really hurts a lot.
There's no more fun in walking, and my dancing's all to pot!
I'm quite subdued.

Oh! Plantar Fasciitis, you're driving me insane,
I never thought a fallen arch could generate such pain.
So take a lesson if you love to walk and run and march,
Be careful not to over-pronate, or you'll get a fallen arch.
And that ain't good.

∞ ∞ ∞ ∞ ∞ ∞ ∞

BALMUCKITY

There was an old dear from Balmuckity
Whose friends found her awfy stuck-uppity.
But she looked really dinkie
As she raised her pinkie
Each time that she sipped from her cuppa-tea.

Jim Smith

THE CYCLE OF LIFE

When I think about this life with all its problems,
  I begin to feel the cycle should be changed.
If we turned it on its head, went from back to front instead,
  We'd be happier that it was re-arranged.

We would start out dead and get that trauma over,
  With the funeral expense out of the way.
In an old folks home we'd languish, with no worries and no anguish,
  And we'd wake up feeling better every day.

Then they'd throw us out for being far too healthy,
  And we'd go collect our pension with a smirk.
Find a nice retirement flat, with a TV and a cat,
  And enjoy life till we're young enough to work.

So we'd find ourselves a job that's to our liking,
  And they'd present us with a gold watch on day one.
Then we'd work for forty years, keeping pace with all our peers,
  Till they let us go away to have some fun.

We'd go home to Mum and Dad for board and lodgings,
  And we'd drink and play the field and have a ball.
When we'd done playing the fool, we'd head off to the High School,
  To get ready for the Primary and all.

Very soon we'd be a child ready for spoiling,
  With birthday parties, toys and treats galore.
And then babyhood would come, with a doting Dad and Mum,
  And we wouldn't have a worry any more.

We would spend our last nine months floating in comfort:
  Central heating and a bigger room each day.
And at the very last, we would go out in a blast
  Of excited adult passion, hip hooray!

∞ ∞ ∞ ∞ ∞ ∞ ∞

BENEATH THE KILT

When the kilted young Gregor McWarder,
Who was travelling south of the border,
    Was asked what was worn
    Beneath kilt and sporran,
He said "Nothing - it's all in good order".

Jim Smith

HOT MILK

The Sisters of Mercy sat round the bed
  Where the Mother Superior lay.
They knew she was dying, nearing the end,
  And they all gathered round her to pray.

One Sister brought her a glass of hot milk,
  It was always her favourite drink.
But she pushed it aside and the Nun went away
  To pour it out into the sink.

But then she remembered the glow they'd all felt
  Last Christmas, when Father McClure
Had secretly brought them, against all the rules,
  Some Irish Cream Whiskey Liqueur.

She searched for the bottle, and found it at last,
  And poured out, as smooth as new silk,
A generous measure into the glass,
  And mixed it in with the hot milk.

Then she carefully cradled the old lady's head,
  And held up the glass to her lips.
When the Mother Superior tasted the drink
  She eagerly took a few sips

The glass was soon drained to the very last drop
  And a brightness came into her eye,
But she said to the Nuns "There's no miracle here,
  For before very long I will die."

The Sisters said "Mother, before you depart
  To live with our God in his kingdom,
Please give us the benefit of some advice
  From your great and superior wisdom."

"Remember your prayers" the old lady said,
  "Keep your vows and be kind to the poor.
Take pride in the Convent, your very own home,
  And look after old Father McClure."

"Take good care of the farm and the animals too,
  The sheep and the goats and the sow."
With a glance at the glass, she said "One final thing,
  Make sure that you don't sell that cow!"

FORFAR

Once an Englishman in a big sports car,
Spiered a loon, "Is there TSB in Forfar?"
        "Naw, jist twa Fs an twa Rs,
        And an O and an A,
Ah'm amazed that ye've fund yir way this far!"

Jim Smith

THE OLD DOG

A dog wandered into my garden one day,
As I sat in the shade of a tree.
Walking straight to my chair, he sat down then and there,
And laid his big head on my knee.

Well I knew what he wanted, so I tickled his ears
And scratched his old belly and back.
How old I can't say, but his whiskers were grey,
Though the rest of his coat was quite black.

When I finished my newspaper I went inside,
And he followed me into the house;
Found a nice quiet place, twirled around in the space,
And slept there as quiet as a mouse.

With ears and legs twitching, he slept for an hour,
Yawned and stretched, and then made for the door.
With scarce a glance round, he was gone, that old hound,
And I thought I would see him no more.

But the very next day, at the very same time,
He came strolling right into my den,
Gave a lick to my face, then found the same place,
And laid down and slept once again.

This went on for some weeks with the same old routine,
He'd come in, take a nap, and then roam.
He was ever so good, never begged me for food,
So I guessed he must have a good home.

Curiosity then got the better of me,
And I knew that I'd have to find out
Just why it should be, that he'd chosen me
As his friend and a place to chill out.

So I put pen to paper and wrote it all down,
Every detail I tried to relate.
In his collar, tucked tight, was the letter that night,
As I ushered him out of the gate.

Still, I feared if they knew where their doggie had been,
They might stop him from roaming so free,
That they might make him stay, at his own house all day,
To prevent him from visiting me.

Well, his mistress was quick to respond to my note:
Her reply came the very next day.
It was witty and smart; writing straight from the heart,
She explained why he wandered away.

She said "I have five kids aged from two up to ten,
And they sure love old Danny alright.
They won't leave him alone, he's no life of his own,
For they plague him from morning till night."

"He's a pony to ride on, a plaything, a pal,
Or a doll to dress up; there's no doubt,
That they take every chance, to lead him a fine dance,
And his patience just never runs out."

"But old Danny, in truth, has a pretty good life,
And you don't have to feel any sorrow.
This is his way to keep catching up on some sleep.
Any chance we could BOTH come to-morrow?"

I met up with his mistress and we soon agreed
It was best not to meddle at all.
We'd let Danny decide where he wanted to hide,
When the children drove him up the wall.

So, old Danny still comes round to see me most days,
When he's at the end of his tether.
He just loves his new bed, and it has to be said,
It's a pleasure to grow old together.

In a way it's like having a grandchild, you know,
All that rare, unconditional love.
They are yours for a while, then go home, and you smile,
It's a match made in heaven above.

SUDOKU

Just position them in grid form, those numbers one to nine,
A challenge when you look at it that seems to be benign,
But when examined deeper, warning bells should start to chime:
Addiction and obsession; stultifying thief of time.

Lost time, lost time, such precious time we never can regain,
Sudoku, oh Sudoku, you could drive a man insane.
Forever one more puzzle, all so different yet the same,
What fiendish oriental mind invented such a game?

ST ANDREWS

In an old boat he bought in St. Andrews,
Jock said "Ah'll sail roon' Fife an' get grand views".
He set sail from Newport,
But sank just off Tayport,
And that put an end to *his* planned cruise.

LADIES IN HEAVEN

Jean and Jessica met up in heaven,
  They were shocked to find each other there.
They'd been best friends for years,
  And they shed lots of tears,
Because dying so young seemed unfair.

Jean said "Jessica, dear, how did you die?"
  And Jess replied "I froze to death".
"Oh how awful" said Jean.
  As she pictured the scene,
She found herself catching her breath.

"Well it wasn't as bad as you'd think, Jean,
  I was shaking with cold for some time,
But then, all warm and tired,
  I just slowly expired,
And the feeling of peace was sublime."

"So what happened to you, Jean", Jess asked her,
  "I'm really quite curious to know.
It's so terribly sad,
  With that winter we've had,
Don't tell me you fell in the snow!"

"I had been to look after my Mother,
  You know that she needs lots of care.
I came home unexpected,
  And quickly suspected
My man had a woman in there."

"When I asked where she was he just grinned back,
  Said my nagging was wearing him thin.
He was so smug and bold,
  That I laid him out cold
With one swipe from the old rolling pin."

"Then I searched the whole house in a frenzy,
  From attic to basement I ran.
Going out of my head,
  I checked under each bed,
While all the time cursing that man."

"I rushed to the garage and store room,
  And the old garden shed out the back,
Till I finally lost it,
  I fell down exhausted,
And I died from a huge heart attack."

Then Jessica wept on Jean's shoulder,
  "It's so tragic we didn't survive,
Had you lifted the lid on
  The freezer I hid in,
There's a chance we'd both still be alive!"

THAT'S WHAT YOU FEEL LIKE DOING

In this life there are so many situations
  That annoy me and frustrate me to the core.
It could be something that's unfair, or someone who doesn't care,
  And I feel I just can't stand it any more.
And I'm sure I would feel better if I faced it:
  Said a few choice words and got it off my chest.
If you get these feelings too, sometimes don't know what to do,
  Here's a few examples of what I think's best.

You rush to town to get a friend's prescription.
  He's feeling desperately under par.
You can't find a place to stop, so you park outside the shop,
  And come out to find a ticket on your car.
And the traffic warden's smirking when he sees you,
  Makes you want to kick his shins and leave him lame.
But you rein your temper in, for you know you wouldn't win,
  Though that's what you feel like doing, just the same.

You go into a pub, it's very crowded,
  And you join the queue to buy a glass of wine.
You stand there patiently, but each time the barman's free,
  He ignores you and serves others in the line.
And you want to shout out loud to the bartender
  "Are you blind, or deaf, or dumb, or just insane?"
But you fight it very hard, for you don't want to be barred,
  Though that's what you feel like doing, just the same.

You receive an invitation to a wedding,
  It's the evening reception, so you go.
You have hardly stepped inside, when your present's laid aside,
  And you're seated beside someone you don't know.
And the 'Band from Hell' is making such a racket
  That you soon begin to wonder why you came.
You can hardly tell the Groom "It's a con", and leave the room.
  But that's what you feel like doing, just the same.

You have set off on that long awaited coach tour,
  To see some sights you've never seen before.
The driver thinks he's it, a comedian, a wit,
  But his constant twitter irks you more and more.
And his stops at 'special' places, 'as a favour'
  Means he's lining his own pockets, that's his game.
You know that if you make a fuss, you'd cause bad feeling on the bus,
  But that's what you feel like doing, just the same.

You are driving through a village in the country,
  Keeping pace with all the vehicles in line.
When out jumps a traffic cop, who beckons you to stop
  And proceeds to talk about a speeding fine.
You get angry and upset and feel like shouting
  That the cars in front were just as much to blame.
But you're heading for the chop if you chin a traffic cop,
  Though that's what you feel like doing, just the same.

So whenever you get in a situation
  Where you feel cheated or aggrieved or fighting mad,
Please try not to start a fight, two wrongs don't make a right,
  And you'd end up feeling miserable and sad.
Count to ten, take a deep breath and speak quite softly,
  Do your utmost to protect your own good name.
There's no lasting satisfaction from extreme or violent action,
  Though that's what you feel like doing, just the same.

THANK YOU FOR MY FAREWELL DINNER

One of the things you had to be punctilious about as a Naval Officer was writing a letter of thanks for any hospitality given as soon as possible afterwards, usually the next day.

It is customary for Officers who are moving on to a new job to be dined out in the Wardroom Mess at the last monthly Mess Dinner before they leave. On this occasion I was serving in HMS COCHRANE at Rosyth, and I was being posted to the Ministry of Defence in London (an appointment not noted for its camaraderie as there is no dedicated accommodation for Naval personnel and therefore no Mess life). My last Mess Dinner at COCHRANE just happened to be on the 24th of January 1975 when they were having a Burns Night celebration.

Instead of a normal letter I wrote these verses to the Wardroom Mess President, Commander Ted Cleland, the following morning. He was kind enough to pin a copy on the Officers' Mess notice board.

The "Royals" referred to are the Band of the Royal Marines, who were based in the Rosyth Dockyard at that time and played their wonderful music at all of our formal Mess Dinners, before and during the meal.

Another point that should be explained is the custom of the officers playing rough physical games in the Ante Room after every formal Mess Dinner (except on Ladies Nights, when we had to be on our best behaviour!). The more senior officers tended to be excused, but the Midshipmen and junior officers always let their hair down and went at it with a will. Sad to say that there were often injuries when some of them got too carried away with enthusiasm! It was always explained as being part of the "work hard, play hard" ethic.

THANK YOU FOR MY FAREWELL DINNER

A favoured chiel am I nae doubt,
For when time came tae dine me out,
The Mess Committee gave a shout
O' joyful glee,
An' paired me wi' that ither lout:
Auld Rabbie B.

At last came roon the Bard's birthnight,
The Mess sat doon by candlelight,
Tae guid Scots fare and – sic delight –
The Famous Grouse,
While Royals blew wi' main an' might
Tae cheer the house.

So, haggis 'dressed, an' Memory paid,
And, dinner over, speeches made,
And thanks tae hosts and staff all said,
Wi' much encore,
Frae there tae Ante-Room we gaed,
Tae revel more.

Ben there the fun went on apace,
Wi' foolish games like 'Horsey Race"
An' still mair Grouse – at least a brace –
Tae cloud ma head,
Until I couldna stand the pace,
An' went tae bed!

And so my friends, when I leave here,
I'll tak wi' me this mem'ry dear,
Tae help in Ministry sae drear,
Tae keep me sane.
Tae all of ye my thanks sincere;
We'll meet again.

Jim Smith

HER SECOND CHANCE

At age thirty-nine, widow Jennifer Jack
Had a sudden and serious heart attack,
And the ambulance took her away.
Sirens blaring, lights flashing, it sped through the town,
And before very long, dressed in surgical gown,
On a hospital trolley she lay.

While the medical experts were doing their best
To relieve the sharp pain that constricted her chest,
Her mind wandered off on its own.
Down a dark narrow tunnel she saw a bright light,
When she finally reached it, there, golden and white,
Was a beautiful ivory throne.

God sat in this chair with his book on his knee,
As she hovered above she could quite plainly see
That her name was right there on the page.
"Oh! don't tell me it's my time, I'm too young to die,
I've just buried my man, now it's my turn to fly,
 There's so much still to do at my age".

Looking up from his book, God said "No, Mrs Jack,
There's quite a long time before I need you back,
I'll just check with my records and see.
Ah, here is the entry, and here's what it says,
You've got thirty-six years, seven months and two days,
Till you come up to heaven to me".

As she slowly recovered, she rested in bed,
But the near-death experience stuck in her head,
And she thought 'This is my second chance.
I will ask to stay on in the hospital wings,
Pay the qualified surgeons to change a few things,
And that might even lead to romance'.

She'd her late husband's money, well that was good luck,
It paid for a face lift and a neat tummy-tuck,
And some liposuction for her hips.
She got pert breast implants that would make the men stare,
Then they whitened her teeth, colour-tinted her hair,
And used Botox to fill out her lips.

When all that was finished, she headed for home,
Impatient to fly out to Paris or Rome,
To find her a rich millionaire.
She flagged down a taxi, and blindly ran out,
Did not even hear the young man's warning shout,
And was killed in the hospital square.

When she got up to heaven she was not amused,
But frustrated and angry and very confused,
So she asked to see God to complain.
St Peter took note but said she'd have to wait,
The list was so long he could not give a date,
Though he saw she was clearly in pain.

When the day came around she confronted her God:
"You promised me long life, but that was a fraud,
My danger you certainly knew.
So why didn't you save me, why not hold me back,
When that ambulance struck?" God said "Dear Mrs Jack,
It's just - I didn't recognise you!"

THE ROBOT

A Dad with a passion for gimmicks and gizmos
  Was browsing a brand new selection,
When he spotted a robot, the shape of a man,
  And its function was strict lie-detection,

"Now this looks like something I really should buy
  To have lots of fun with", he said,
"For it's programmed that when it discovers a liar,
  It gives them a slap on the head".

Well, he paid lots of money and took it straight home,
  And it fair fitted in with the rest.
So when everyone sat down to dinner that night
  He decided to give it a test.

He asked his son Charlie what he'd done that day,
  And he said "Just schoolwork, I fear".
At that point the Robot, with obvious glee,
  Gave Charlie a slap on the ear.

"OK, I watched movies at my best friend's house"
  And Dad then said, "which one, my son?"
"Toy Story" said Charlie, and quick as a flash,
  The Robot slapped his other one.

"OK, OK, we were watching some porn",
  Said young Charlie, by this time in tears.
"If that's what you're up to" said Dad in disgust,
  "You deserve both those slaps on your ears."

"When I was your age I was such a good boy
  Not one image of that stuff I saw."
And that's when the Robot raced round the table,
  And gave Dad a right slap on the jaw!

"Well he's certainly your son, he takes after you",
  Said Mum with a laugh and a grin.
The Robot was straight back in action again,
  And gave Mum a slap on the chin!

So Dad took that Robot and locked it away,
  And that is the end of my tale,
Except, nobody speaks in that house any more,
  And the Robot's on e-Bay, 'For Sale'.

∞ ∞ ∞ ∞ ∞ ∞ ∞

FRIOCKHEIM

A redoubtable spinster from Friockheim,
Said "just find me a man and I'll tweak him"
    But all she could get
    (and she's stuck with him yet)
Was a drunk with a nose like a beacon.

Jim Smith

TO SAY OR NOT TO SAY

It's a fact that our language is changing,
  With new words and new phrases each year,
While it's handy for 'Scrabble',
Some words are just babble,
  And sound very strange to the ear.

For they aren't the words we grew up with,
  We'd no twitter, no blog and no tweet.
Now there's rumping and munchy,
LOL, lashed and scrunchy,
  And some more words I daren't repeat.

Well, I don't mind some new words appearing
  But I hope things don't get out of hand,
For the last thing we need
When we sit down to read
  Is to see words we don't understand.

It's too easy for standards to falter,
  And for words to get changed on the way.
If you don't believe it,
Here's how I perceive it
  In the case of the old verb 'to say'.

When I was at school it was simple,
  There were tenses which showed us the way.
In the past tense we'd *'he said'*,
And *'we said'* and *'she said'*,
  In the present we just said *'I say'*.

But hearing them speak down in London,
 Would have near brought a tear to your eye.
They'd say 'I sez' and ' she sez',
No matter wot 'e sez',
 And sometimes 'twas 'I sez, sez I'.

Then, returning from work one fine evening,
 On the train, which was packed, by the way,
I was taken aback,
As we sped down the track,
 To hear two girls discussing their day.

They were talking about conversations
 In which no-one was 'saying' a thing:
It was 'I went' and 'she went'
And 'they went' and 'he went'
 To my ears it had a strange ring.

And then they changed tense to the present,
 Though their story was still in the past,
It was 'I go' and 'she goes'
And 'they go' and 'he goes',
 And I thought 'this queer language won't last'.

But soon the fad gathered momentum,
 And in less than a decade or so,
That nice little word,
Though it does seem absurd,
 Had been changed from' I say' to 'I go'.

But that's not the end of the story,
  For before many more years had gone,
Another new way
To express the word 'say'
  Was beginning to grow and catch on.

When I heard it I couldn't believe it,
  For it wasn't 'to say' or 'to go',
It was *'I'm like'* and *'she's like'*
And *'they're like'* and *'he's like'*
  And what it meant I didn't know.

But soon it was there all around us,
  On the TV and radio too.
And comedians all strive
To keep it alive,
  But I wish it would founder, don't you?

Let us hope that this verb is safeguarded,
  In the future: no changes we pray.
No more *'he's like'* or *'he goes'*,
Or *'she's like'* or *'she goes'*,
  But simply just you and I - *'say'.*

I'VE WORKED IT OUT

I have a dog, a sleazy hound, he sleeps ten hours a day,
His meals are all prepared for him, with never a penny to pay.
He lives in a decent neighbourhood, in a house that's far too big.
He doesn't help with its upkeep, and he doesn't care a fig.

He's had his choice of luxury beds since he was just a pup,
And when he makes a mess of things, there's someone to clear it up,
He sees his doctor once a year for his regular health check,
And any time that he gets ill, does he pay? Does he heck!

He's happiest meeting people and he'll 'give a paw' all day.
He'll eat their treats and have no qualms that they're the ones who pay.
He fair enjoys his lush lifestyle, it's absolutely free,
And everyone admires him, so he lives like royalty.

The only thing he's good at, and even this may be 'pretend',
Is to shine when he's in company and be everybody's friend.
I've often wondered how he got this enviable position,
Then it hit me like a ton of bricks:- My dog's a Politician!

Jim Smith

SUCCESS

We hope to be successful as we travel on life's way,
Good school reports, a fine degree, a job with lots of pay,
A really happy marriage, clever children, girl and boy,
Nice house in a good neighbourhood, a garden to enjoy.

Status in the community and money in the bank,
A swimming pool, a real smart car, with fuel in the tank,
If we had the good fortune to achieve all that, I guess,
We'd all be quite delighted with those symbols of success.

But there are other markers of success that we can find,
A few of them are physical and some are in our mind,
We measure them as life progresses through its different stages,
And recognise them easily at some specific ages.

At three years old we know among the many cans and cants,
The real grown-up success sign is **not peeing in your pants,**
And when we arrive at teenage we know success depends,
On being very popular and **having lots of friends.**

At seventeen we know in life we won't get very far,
Until we pass that **licence test to let us drive a car,**
And all grown up at twenty, when we know we know it all,
Success is **having lots of sex** and standing really tall.

By thirty-five we hope we've found our land of milk and honey,
For at that point in middle age success means **lots of money,**
And so we get to forty when our life begins anew,
What's gone around then comes around, it's oh so very true.

Involved with work and family throughout our middle age,
Each day brings something different as we strut upon life's stage,
We struggle on to sixty-five, it really isn't funny,
That we're still gauging our success as having *lots of money.*

Then we retire and things reverse, our life begins to pall,
We claim success at seventy-five *if we have sex at all!*
At eighty years we want our independence, nothing less,
To still have our driving licence is our measure of success.

At eighty-five we've been through all life's many twists and bends,
And at that ripe old age success is *having any friends,*
But of all the great successes we achieve as life decants,
The pinnacle at ninety is, *not peeing in your pants!*

∞ ∞ ∞ ∞ ∞ ∞ ∞

MONTROSE

A young farmer wi' dung on his clothes
Tried tae chat up a lass in Montrose.
When he said "How's yersel?"
She said "No very well,
Wi' the stink o' your coos up ma nose".

ALL THIS CHANGE

When I examine all the change that's in my pocket,
It makes me sad that just one monarch's head appears.
That's no reflection on the Queen,
Who is the best there's ever been,
But I yearn to see a few from former years.

Looking back in time, around the nineteen-fifties,
We would have found this situation very strange.
Then you could safely guarantee,
That many Kings and Queens you'd see,
When you dipped into your pocket for some change.

Older coins were then in common circulation,
And we would recognise each face like an old friend:
Two King Georges and an Edward with
Queens Victoria and Elizabeth,
Kept us company when we went out to spend.

Just by reading all those dates on coins as children,
We knew the years each King and Queen was on the throne,
So we had no need to be taught,
Because we used them such a lot,
And we worked out all those details on our own.

To me the coins were absolutely fascinating,
They had so many different symbols on the tails:
Ships and Shields and Crowns were there,
Plus proud Britannia on her chair,
And the flowers of England, Scotland, Ireland, Wales.

Even though mere humble coins, they had their value,
All those farthings, pennies, threepennys, tanners, bobs,
And if of that you've any doubt,
Ask any former, keen Boy Scout,
Who helped raise funds by doing neighbours' "bob-a-jobs"

Now, the basis of our ancient money system,
Is the Troy silver scale of precious metal weight:
In twelve Troy Ounces to the Pound,
240 pennyweights are found,
So, for £. s. d. you just extrapolate.

And for centuries it served us very nicely,
With gradual changes to the various coins we used,
Crowns and Sovereigns, Guineas, Groats,
Paper pounds and ten-bob notes,
Were good for us, although the tourists were confused.

But when computers came along there was a problem,
For they just couldn't cope with pounds, shillings and pence.
Vulgar fractions were aberration,
So in came decimalisation,
And I suppose, from that viewpoint, it all made sense.

They didn't ask for my advice, I wrote and told them,
That the Chancellor should be practical and bold,
He should make our pound much smaller,
More like the value of the Dollar,
Then he could give us two new pounds for every old.

And another good idea I advocated,
Was to reduce our coins from seven down to four.
In North America they survive,
With one, five, ten and twenty-five,
It's the simplest in the world, you don't need more.

Then revaluing our coins would be straightforward,
And the baby not thrown out with the bath-water.
Five new pence for the old tanner,
And by progression in like manner:
The shilling would be ten, the half-crown quarter.

This would mean we could retain most of our old coins,
Alongside new ones coming out in steady flow.
These could be phased in year by year,
And that would not be half as dear,
As minting billions of the new coins at one go.

But what did I know about high finance and money?
And who was I to bother Ministers with letters?
I ought to learn to keep my place,
And not expect them to lose face,
And leave decisions to my elders and my betters.

Yes, these decisions have to come from politicians,
And they don't always get it right, that's what I've found,
It really wasn't a stone-waller,
They could have made our unit smaller,
But they stubbornly hung on to the 'Big' Pound.

So with each penny now worth two-and-a-half old ones,
The cost of living took a meteoric rise.
Despite the MPs' protestation,
That it wouldn't cause inflation,
It surely did, which caused the public no surprise.

Well, the new coins all appeared in quick succession,
And then the older coins were very soon withdrawn,
Until the only head to be seen,
Was just Elizabeth, the Queen,
And those old friendly royal faces had all gone.

So now whenever I take change out of my pocket,
I can't help thinking that it would have been so grand,
To keep that old link with the past,
Alas, it disappeared too fast,
And I miss holding all that history in my hand.

Sometimes I feel that it is more than pure nostalgia,
For my lost youth and things I used to love back then,
But time has come to draw a line,
I must convince myself - "it's fine",
For those old coins are never coming back again.

TROON

A lassie ca'd Cassie frae Troon
Gave her all tae McCall frae Dunoon
First he said 'it's true love',
Then he gave her the shove,
She's in pain, and his wean's comin' soon.

SHEFFIELD '96

(My one and only attempt at writing in the Yorkshire Dialect)

The Speakers 'eld a Conference, they came from near and far,
  Some came to Sheffield by train and bus, and some by motor car,
But before inside the Cutlers' Hall they were allowed to look,
  Each had to go and register, to tick off name in t'book.
They wandered round the lovely halls wi' lots of oohs and aahs,
  Then back to t'hotel to freshen up, and check out all the bars.

The Friday were Mikado Night, when all the girls and chaps
  Got dressed up in kimonos and pretended they were Japs.
"Three little maids" were 'murdered' half a dozen times or more,
  And the Lord High Executioner tried to even up the score.
The Topics Competition was a useful intermission,
  And Trevor Millar winning proved a popular decision.

The Lord Mayor opened AGM wi' eloquence and wit,
  And after t'Mayor had gone 'ome came t'usual Conference bit.
Wi' sederunts an' minutes an' votes about the levy,
  Elections, motions an' reports, an' eyelids gettin' 'eavy.
Till a fiery lass, wi' a voice like brass, tried her tale to tell,
  But she were out of order, an' soon out the door as well!

After lunch they'd seminars to make them try and think
  How to increase the membership, an' drag them back from t'brink.
Then, highlight of the afternoon, came t'annual speech contest,
  Wi' eight contestants from all ower, North, South, East an' West.
By telling them how Scots just love in nostalgia to wallow,
  Willie Erskine won the cup, he'll be a hard act to follow.

At night they 'ad the Dinner Dance, all dressed up in their best,
  The food were great and t'after dinner speakers stood the test.
The raffle raised a princely sum and t'prizes all were won,
  So then they 'ad the dancing to complete the evening's fun.
They'd waltzes, jives an' quicksteps, an' the wine went to their 'eads,
  It all went on past midnight, when they staggered to their beds.

Up i' the morning wi' the lark for unusual Sunday service,
  Wi' Whiston Band to help out any singer that were nervous.
Brendan Power then made the speech for t'Evaluation Contest,
  An' again they had competitors from East, South, North an' West.
Eight different evaluators gave it their best try,
  But it were Linda Hodgkinson that took the judges' eye.

Then Ken Sharpe closed proceedings, saying how much e'd enjoyed
  The company, and the business that had kept them all employed.
He felt they were all in good heart, an' said e'd every reason
  To think they could look forward to a most successful season.
He wished them all safe journey 'ome and 'oped they'd 'ave the sense
  To make their way to Glasgow, for next year's Conference.

Jim Smith

IN MEMORIAM

Our King is dead! He was our dearest friend;
  We scarcely can believe his life has passed.
He showed his greatest faith before his end;
  'Twas in his noblest hour he breathed his last.

To all his people he was ever fair,
  His understanding showed in many ways:
He gave his all to us, and we did share
  His happiness, but not his saddest phase.

He overcame his weakness, hid his pain,
  And gave his country hope in darkest day,
But all his gallant efforts were in vain,
  His toil-worn body yielded to the fray.

He had no son to hear the Nation's call:
"The King is dead! Long Live the Queen", say all.

I wrote this little sonnet in 1952 when King George VI died, and it was printed in the School Magazine.

On re-reading it now, I don't think it is the best thing I've ever done, but it is interesting that the weakness I mentioned in the third verse (his stammer) should be the subject of the recent blockbuster film starring Colin Firth and Helena Bonham Carter, which painted a memorable picture of this kind, gentle and thoroughly decent man who had kingship thrust upon him.

ADDRESS TO GOLF

Hail! ancient, royal, Scottish game.
How proud we are tae mak' the claim
That frae this land ye ca' yir hame,
      Yir land o' birth,
Tae gaither international fame
      Ye ventured forth.

Ne'er thocht yon ancient, on that day,
Wha, just tae pass the time away
Tried hittin' chuckies ower the clay
      Wi' crookit stick,
That ither loons wad want tae play,
      An' catch on quick.

Soon, wi' wee gowfba's made o' leather,
An stappit fu' wi' bits o' feather,
Men trampit ower the links thegither,
      Playin' tae win.
Rain, hail or snaw, despite the weather,
      Ha'ein' their fun.

They made their clubs wi' hickory sticks,
Drivers, brassies, putters, cleeks,
Niblicks an mashies tae gi'e the ba' wheeks
      An' get guid scores.
They even invented special breeks,
      Plus twos an' fours!

Courses sprang up a' aroon',
St Andrews, Carnoustie, Gullane, Troon.
'Til every self respectin' toon
    Its ain course built.
They've even got wan on the moon,
    Or so Ah'm telt!

An' noo we're here in modern day.
The game's progressed in every way.
The graphite shaft's come into play,
    That mak's ba's flee,
Ower the rough an' far away,
    Tae green, frae tee.

It's widely kent Scots love all sport.
On football pitch or tennis court,
Or curling rink, where they disport
    Tae hurl a stane.
But naethin' beats oor best export,
    GOLF is the game!

The Poet's Personal PS

Although we're here in modern day,
An' the game's progressed in every way,
Wi' graphite shafts by Callaway
    An' ba's that flee
Ower the rough an' far away:
    But no' for me!

I slice an' hook an' sclaff the grun,
I shank an' duff, it's no' much fun,
My stance is odd, my grip's undone,
    My game's a mess.
I can't remember when I last won,
    Last year, I guess.

It's all so sad, my bell won't ring.
But, hope is an amazing thing,
Just one long putt or one great swing
    Will see me back.
Wi' balls by Top Flite, putter by Ping,
    I'll gie it a crack!

ADDRESS TO GOLF

*(A translation into English for those that
find the Scottish Dialect difficult to follow)*

Hail! ancient, royal, Scottish game.
How proud we are to make the claim
That from this realm that made your name,
    Your land of birth,
To gather international fame
    You ventured forth.

Never thought that ancient, on that day,
Who, just to pass the time away,
Tried hitting pebbles o'er the clay
    With crooked stick,
That other lads would want to play,
    And catch on quick.

Soon, with wee golf balls made of leather,
And packed real tight with bits of feather,
Men traipsed across the links together,
    Playing to win.
Rain, hail or snow, despite the weather,
    Having their fun.

They made their clubs with hickory sticks,
Drivers, brassies, putters, cleeks,
Niblicks and mashies to give the ball licks
    And get good scores.
They even invented special breeks,
    Plus Twos and Fours!

Golf courses sprang up everywhere,
St Andrews, Carnoustie, Gullane, Ayr,
And every town with cash to spare
     Built one right soon.
Even Outer Space - they've got one there -
     It's on the moon!

So now we're here in modern day,
The game's progressed in every way,
The graphite shaft's come into play,
     That makes balls soar
Over the rough to the fairway
     While we shout 'fore'.

It's widely known Scots love all sport.
On football pitch or tennis court,
Or curling rink, where they disport
     To hurl a stone.
But nothing beats our best export,
     GOLF is *the* one!

OH! WHY CAN'T THE ENGLISH?

Oh! why can't the English say wh?
The H just disappears, it's too bad
That they don't seem to care, that their 'wot', 'wen' and 'ware'
Should be what, when and where, it's so sad.

And sometimes I get quite perplexed,
By the way they enthuse about Wales
Swimming under the sea, that sounds crazy to me,
Ah, but then, they're referring to whales!

And my mind gets a little confused
Every time that they say the word 'wich'.
Was she burned at the stake? or is this a mistake?
And they really were just saying which?

Oh! I wish they would learn to say wh,
I'm so fed up with 'wisper' and 'wite'.
And it gives me the needle when they 'wimper' and 'weedle',
But I'll try not to get too uptight.

Oh! why can't the English say och ?
When they try the H changes to K.
It's 'ock aye the noo' and 'lock Lomond' too,
It's so funny to hear what they say.

But it's not only Scots that use ch,
And it's not just a modern trend:
Every Arab and Jew, and I've met quite a few,
Has an Achmed or Malachi friend.

And the Germans, they use it a lot,
In their everyday speech it abounds,
You'll hearAchtung and hoch and Ich Bien and koch,
They don't mind making guttural sounds.

So, come on you English, and try,
It's not as hard as you make out.
Close your tongue at the back and force wind through the crack,
You'll be oching before the day's out.

Oh! why can't the English say rrrrr ?
It's as if all their tongues have no tips.
So, while every proud Scot rolls his Rs quite a lot,
They just can't get a rrrrr past their lips.

If an R's at the start of a word,
They can make quite a passable sound.
With their tongues at the top, they just let their jaws drop,
And it comes out like (R)oger, or (R)ound.

So, in most cases R disappears,
(And this is not meant as a slur),
They just throw in the towel, and lengthen the vowel,
And say 'ga.....den', or' ha.....bour', or fu.....

But, when the words end with an A,
They throw in an R everywhere:
It's KenyaRand ChinaRand EmmaRand InaR,
AmericaRAfricaRAsiaRAustralia',
Rs ad infinitum, I'm left in despair!

THE NON-WORKIN' CLASS

Ye're bound tae huv seen him struttin' doon the street,
Wi' his shouders rockin' an' his big splash feet
Decked oot in new trainers by Addidas.
It's only the best fur the non-workin' class.

In designer blue jeans an' a fitba shurt,
His heid shaved sae close that it must huv hurt,
Smokin' a roll-up that might even be grass,
That's the uniform o' the non-workin' class.

He's the third generation on the dole,
But claims we're tae blame that he's in this hole,
Thae exams that we didnae let him pass,
That's why he belongs tae the non-workin' class.

Well, it's a' haunded doon frae faither tae son,
How tae wangle the system, tae them it's great fun,
They ken every angle, it's a' clear as glass,
Aye, ye huv tae be fly when ye're non-workin' class

Nae Spaniel fur him, nae Collie, nae Pug,
Naw, he's oot paradin' his Staffie dug,
Jist demonstratin' tae a' them that pass,
His status symbol o' the non-workin' class.

He gi'es Staffie's lead a right vicious tug,
An' then claps his mobile phone tae his lug,
Makin' contact wi' his current live-in lass.
Ye've at least wan o' them when ye're non-workin' class.

He shouts doon the phone she's tae come an' meet him,
He's nae benefits left, so she'll huv tae treat him,
An' keep the bairns safe mind, use the underpass.
Every kid means mair cash fur the non-workin' class.

They arrive an' he shows them his latest tattoo,
O' a Kiltie weildin' a big skean dubh.
Tae huv nae body art wid be downright crass,
Ye've tae keep up appearances as non-workin' class.

She's spent the week's rent, God knows where it's gone,
But they could raise some cash if they'd somethin' tae pawn,
Och, jist let's try the Food Bank says he, bold as brass,
Well, ye still huv tae eat though ye're non-workin' class.

You'll find them in each and every city,
They won't work nor want, it's such a great pity.
That things hud tae come tae this terrible pass:
Fully three generations o' non-workin' class.

AIRLIE

A careless auld mannie frae Airlie,
Chawed doon on an aipple ower sairlie,
His false teeth broke in twa,
An' he swallowed them a',
Noo his wife says he's feelin' fell pairlie.

THE WINE TASTING

Jack and Nellie were invited by the Wine Club
  To a tasting at a very posh hotel.
With his best suit on his back,
And with Nellie smart in black,
  They strolled into the venue looking swell.

But they soon began to feel quite out of place there,
  When the members rolled up in a burst of noise,
Sporting wide-brimmed leather hats,
Fancy shirts and loud cravats,
  Coloured jackets, polo necks, and corduroys.

Then the Chairman said he'd take them on a journey
  Round the world of wines, to countries north and south.
That they'd learn to tell the best
From the mediocre rest,
  With their eyes and nose and finally their mouth.

First the members would take turns at the descriptions,
  And pronounce their verdict on each white and red.
They would sniff and sip and savour,
To diagnose the flavour,
  And Jack and Nell would learn from all they said.

But they took so long in getting down to business,
  Kept them waiting for the samples, hints and tips,
That Jack said "Nellie, my old flower,
We've been here for near an hour,
  And not a ruddy drop has passed our lips!"

But then finally the corks began a-popping,
  And the wines in shades of white went on parade.
The first one on the go,
Italian Pinot Grigio,
  Was so welcome it went down like lemonade.

The first man thought it 'delicate' and 'zesty',
  With hints of olive, almond, pear and plum.
But Nellie felt that it was 'thin',
Said she'd much prefer a gin,
  And began to fret and wish she hadn't come.

But the next one up was much more to her liking,
  A sunny Californian Chardonnay.
In a stunning shade of yellow,
It tasted soft and mellow,
  So she drank it down and said that she would stay.

Then the member in the paisley-patterned waistcoat,
  Did his tasting and pronounced it rather fine.
Said that they should really savour
All that tropical fruit flavour,
  Zestful melon and pineapple – so divine.

And its lovely lime and guava middle palate,
  Leading on to hints of butterscotch and cream
And freshly buttered toast,
That's what he had liked the most.
  Made Jack wonder when he'd wake up from his dream!

Then they zipped across the ocean to Australia,
  For a cheeky little Riesling, crisp and dry,
Which, the member with the wig,
As she downed another swig,
  Said she'd recommend as just the one to buy.

With its characters of lemon, lime and grapefruit,
  Cool and tart, with just the merest hint of peach,
She said "it's great with spicy food,
And it's equally as good
  At a "Barbie" in the garden or the beach".

Next, the man in desert boots and baggy trousers
  Described a wine he thought especially nice.
It was a fine reserve Shiraz,
Full of pepper and pizzazz,
  With the heady smells of liquorice and spice.

And, exploding on the tongue, ripe blackberry and plum
  With hints of smoky chocolate eclair.
Nellie whispered "these folk here
Have got verbal diarrhoea,
  And the sad thing is, none of them seem to care!"

And then she said "I'm puzzled by these wine buffs,
  I see that some don't even like the taste:
For after every sup,
They spit it out into a cup,
  And they never drink the sample – what a waste!"

"And then there is that constant repetition
  About fruits of all varieties and shapes,
What with pears and plums and apples,
Pomegranates and pineapples,
  I wonder how there's any room for grapes!"

At last the Chairman had his say about a Merlot:
  How it opened with sweet mulberry in the nose,
And the soft vanilla base
Had put a smile upon his face.
  A great choice to bring the evening to a close.

"I would recommend this vintage to the members",
  You should buy it now before you leave this place,
With its bright rich ruby hue,
This is just the wine for you,
  And it's a bargain at a hundred pounds a case!"

"Now, next month we'll have another grand selection
  To let you demonstrate your expertise:
Malbec from the Argentine
And Neirsteiner from the Rhine,
  With some great Champagne to put you at your ease."

And his voice droned on reciting from his wine list
  As Nell and Jack retreated through the door.
She said "I'm glad we're off that hook"
And he said "Take one final look,
  For we won't be going back there any more."

Jim Smith

I came home late one Sunday night from weekend sea training with the RNVR. Everyone was in bed, but there was a note on the mantelpiece from my Dad saying that the Budgie had died. He had put it in a little cardboard box by the sink, and said he would get the younger children to bury it in the garden the next day. I wrote this wee poem before going to bed and left it on the mantelpiece for them to find in the morning. I was sixteen at that time.

ON THE PASSING AWAY OF OUR BUDGIE

Och pair wee burd, ye're lyin' there sae quate,
An' sic a transformation in that tiny form,
The words are stickin', ah can hardly say it,
Ye're deid! And you wis aye sae live an' warm.

The cage that's ower yonner at the wa,
Is shairly no the same sine ye're no there,
There's nae denyin' that the cage is braw,
But, sine vacated, it looks cauld an' bare.

Ah'm wondrin', if ye hadna lost yer mate,
Wad ye be livin' yet, an' singin' still?
Or wad ye, by some devilish touch o' fate,
Be lyin' there in death's last cruel chill?

The bairns will miss ye an' yer cheerful sang,
Yer chirpin' an' yer antics on the swing,
Yer memory will bide wi' us ower lang,
Oh death! Thou shairly art a heartless thing.

This blow brings hame tae us the bitter thought,
That all guid things canna forever last,
So we shall mourn yer death, as mourn we ought,
An' then look furrit, an' forget the past.

WOMAN

When God set out to make a mate
  For Adam, his new man,
He thought of lots of attributes
  And made a perfect plan.

A finer head than Adam's,
  With hair in the right place.
Two eyes, two ears, a button nose
  Adorning a sweet face.

A nicely rounded body,
  With curves in fullest measure.
A full and ample bosom,
  With two breasts for added pleasure.

Two shapely legs to catch his eye
  And help her cast her spell.
Two good strong arms to do the work
  And dextrous hands as well.

There was no finer creation,
  In east, west, north or south.
But then God went and spoiled it all,
  By giving her - a mouth.

THE W.C.

In the summer of nineteen hundred and two,
When the century was still brand new,
A retired headmistress, Evangeline Pugh,
    Was trying to find,
A suitable holiday room with a view,
    With the future in mind.

She had made some arrangements well in advance,
Then she travelled the length and breadth of France,
Till she stumbled across it, somewhat by chance,
    Quite hidden away,
In that land full of beauty and love and romance,
    A superb place to stay.

The village was tranquil, with no sign of care,
It had several shops, and a house for 'Le Maire',
And white-painted dwellings surrounding the square,
    Yet still there was space,
For the Saturday crowds that would congregate there,
    In the quaint market place.

The local schoolmaster, Jacques, showed her around,
It was clear that her needs would not simply be found,
But they finally went to a house on high ground,
    With a room looking out
On the beautiful valley with vineyards all round,
    This was it, she'd no doubt.

She met with the landlord and booked right away,
And then returned home, it took more than a day,
And when her friends asked, she was happy to say,
    "It really suits me".
But she couldn't remember, try as she may,
    Seeing a W.C.

Well, her bladder could not withstand long deprivation,
And knowing the horrors of French sanitation,
She wrote to Jacques asking for his confirmation,
    Of a toilet close by.
Then she waited for ages in anticipation
    Of a helpful reply.

At colloquial English Jacques wasn't too grand,
When he read 'W.C.' he did not understand,
So he went to the Priest with the letter in hand,
    Who said "W.C.?"
"Must mean that Wayside Chapel a few miles inland,
    That's what it must be."

Then Jacques wrote back saying "Dear Mademoiselle,
In response to your letter I'm happy to tell,
There's a fine W.C. near the old wishing-well,
    Just four miles away.
It is open on Sundays, and Thursdays as well,
    And there's nothing to pay.

So please, my dear mademoiselle, do not despair,
We can order a carriage to zoom you out there,
Or a pony and trap if that's what you prefer,
    When it's sunny and bright.
But the road is quite bumpy, so we'll say a prayer,
    That you get there alright.

There are two hundred seats, filled for most of the year.
The acoustics are great, every sound we all hear.
And a recent donation, that filled us with cheer,
    Was a bell, which we chose.
Every time someone goes it rings out loud and clear
    So that everyone knows!

This W.C. with its classic design,
Is set in a wood of spruce, alder and pine,
You must book in advance, or you could stand in line
    For an hour or so.
But the trees give good shelter, and we'd all say "Fine",
    If you just had to go.

My wife has a problem, she's a delicate one,
She can't go regularly, it isn't much fun,
It's been nearly a year now, and she weighs a ton,
    And suffers much pain.
But I'm happy that now it is her intention,
    To go once again.

We have held a bazaar to raise funds for some new
Padded seats for us all, it's the least we can do.
I'd be pleased to book *the* very best one for you,
    Dear Mademoiselle,
You'll be right at the front and we'll all get a view,
    Of you ringing the bell.

Well, needless to say, Miss Pugh wasn't impressed,
And with her ailing bladder she thought it was best.
To abandon her French plans and head to the west,
    At a right cracking pace,
So she hopped on a train to put Wales to the test,
    As a holiday place.

When she reached Aberystwyth on Cardigan Bay,
Saw the prom, and the beach, and the children at play,
And the fine public toilets, with nothing to pay,
    Even out on the pier,
She thought:- 'This is a place, I could easily stay,
    For most of the year'.

In a big beachfront dwelling, she found a fine room,
Where glorious sunsets dispelled any gloom,
And, wonder of wonders, an en-suite bathroom,
    Her own W.C.!
With no crowds to watch her, and no four-mile zoom,
    When she needed a pee.

∞ ∞ ∞ ∞ ∞ ∞ ∞

KILRY

(Pronounced KILLray)

There was a young lassie from Kilry,
Who hated her name, which was Jill Rae,
    But she said "It will change,
    When I wed", so it's strange,
That she married a laddie called Bill Rae.

(and if you want to add a second verse,
which is most unusual for a Limerick)

So her name hasn't changed, it is still Rae,
And it's worse than when she was just Jill Rae,
    For now when they go out,
    All the bairns laugh and shout,
"There go Bill Rae and Jill Rae frae Kilry".

THE LIFE OF MAN

When God settled down to commence his creating,
He pondered how long each new creature should live,
As the wrong length of life might be exasperating,
An appropriate lifespan He felt He should give.

He examined the dog and said "You're a bright spark,
Ideal to guard houses by night and by day,
I will give you sharp teeth and a very loud bark,
And a menacing growl to keep villains at bay."

"I suggest twenty years you should sit at the door,
And bark at each one who walks past or comes in."
But the dog said "I'd find that too much of a chore,
All that snarling and barking and making a din."

"Could you shorten my life to about fifteen years,
And take back the five to distribute elsewhere?"
God relented, not wanting to see dog in tears,
And He held back the balance to keep as a spare.

God then turned to the monkey, a playful wee thing,
He was so acrobatic and quick as a dart,
He could run, he could climb, jump and tumble and swing,
And his cheeky expression just melted God's heart.

"With your tricks you could entertain people all day,
An excellent job for a monkey to do,
Folks will laugh at your antics whenever you play,
Twenty years of this fun I will allocate you."

"Twenty years is too long to perform monkey tricks,
Could you please take off five? like you did for the dog."
Whereupon God replied "Right, that's easy to fix,
And I may use those five for a frog, or a hog."

Then he looked at the cow, its potential was great,
"You would be such a help in man's journey through life,
You could work for the farmer from morning till late,
Bring forth calves and give milk for his children and
wife."

"When your life's work is over, magnificent beast,
Your hide will make leather for clothing and shoes,
And your flesh will provide such a succulent feast,
You shall have sixty years, I hope you don't refuse."

But the cow was aghast, saying "Sixty's a lot,
That's too tough a prospect you're offering me,
But I'd labour for twenty and give all I've got",
And so God took back forty, and said "I agree"

Then God spoke to Adam, his special creation,
"You're made in my image, so you shall stand tall,
I'll give you a good life to match your new station,
You shall have special privilege over them all."

"You can sleep, eat and play all the days of your life,
Get married, have children and live without fears,
In this idyllic lifestyle both you and your wife,
Will in happiness live for a full twenty years."

But Adam was sure that was not enough time,
To do all the things running round in his head,
He did not want to die at the height of his prime,
So he asked God a favour, and here's what he said.

"You could add the dog's five, plus the monkey's, and then
Throw in the odd forty the cow has refused,
That would give me a lifespan of three score and ten".
And God gave him his wish though it left Him bemused.

It's as if God foresaw all those long years ago,
The outcome of Adam's spontaneous plan,
How the long-term effects of 'you reap what you sow',
Would impact on the life-style of modern-day man.

For the first twenty years he just plays, eats and sleeps,
Sings and parties and dances, and cuts a fine dash,
But when marriage and children bring problems in heaps,
He must find good employment to bring in the cash.

For the next forty years he slaves hard in the sun,
To put food and drink on the table each day,
He works and he worries till his life's nearly done,
And then when he retires for his long holiday.

He amuses grandchildren for five years or more,
With cute monkey tricks and a silly old grin,
Then he sits on his front porch till his life is o'er,
And just barks at all those who walk past or come in.

ROBERT STEWART

Extempore vote of thanks in rhyme to
Robert Stewart of Kirriemuir
for his talk on completion of his year in office
as President of
The Robert Burns World Federation.

18 December 2013 at the Thrums Hotel, Kirriemuir.

Oh! Bob, you've had a busy year,
You've travelled far and wide,
With mony a laugh, and maybe a tear
Shed round the countryside.
You've spoken here, you've spoken there,
And opened mony a door.
There isn't any doubt you've been
A great ambassador.

A FISHY TAIL

A few years ago there was a series of letters in our daily newspaper about rhyming in poetry.

People were divided into two camps. One maintained that all rhymes had to be perfect, while the other felt that it was acceptable to make approximate rhymes which sound right when said aloud.

Much was made of several words, including 'silver', for which there is no known rhyme. Some readers thought that it is cheating to use lookalike words that don't sound the same, such as 'bone' and 'none' in Old Mother Hubbard.

Although I always get great satisfaction from finding the perfect rhyme, I am not unhappy with imperfect ones, especially since I believe that poetry is meant to be read aloud. So I sent in the following limerick, which they printed.

Strangely, the correspondence stopped dead in the water!

> While out fishing, young Robert Da Silva,
> Saw a quick flash of something like silver,
>   He thought "Salmon or Trout?"
>   But when he pulled it out
> It was only a common young elver.

About the Author

Jim Smith was born in Glasgow in 1934 and educated at Knightswood School and Allan Glen's School. Always keen on being a sailor, he became a member of the Volunteer Reserve in 1950, eventually joining the Royal Navy as a Writer at the age of 18. He went on to serve for 34 years, working his way up to the rank of Commander by the age of 43. During his career he served in Frigates, Destroyers and Submarine Depot Ships in UK, Mediterranean, Persian Gulf, Far Eastern, Caribbean and South American waters. He also saw shore service in England, Scotland and Bahrain, as well as Denmark where he served with NATO.

He married Muriel in Kirriemuir in 1960. They now have two grown-up sons, one married to a Russian girl and one married to an Irish girl, and they have two grandsons.

On leaving the Navy in 1986, he spent several years as Development Manager of the old wooden warship, The Frigate Unicorn, at Dundee before leaving to buy a shop in Arbroath. He finally retired to Muriel's home town of Kirriemuir in 1993. Since then they have travelled extensively on holidays, but always keeping busy in the local community.

Jim has been Chairman of the Trustees of his local community hall, the Northmuir Hall, since 1997 and together with Muriel runs a weekly Tea Dance and fortnightly Whist Drives there. They are also involved with the fledgling Kirriemuir and District Burns and Scottish Literary Society, which is growing in popularity and helping to promote interest in four of Scotland's historic literary figures – Burns, Barrie, Scott and Stevenson as well as more recent writers. Jim is also a Past President of the Kirriemuir Probus Club and a private member of the Robert Burns World Federation.

Jim's main hobby has been Public Speaking since joining the Association of Speakers Clubs in 1982. He has been President of Speakers Clubs in Dunfermline, Dundee and Kirriemuir, and also at North Tay Area and Northern District levels.

He won the UK National Speech Contest at Buxton in 1985 and was a national finalist again in 1995 and 2002. He remains heavily involved with the Strathmore Speakers Club and chaired a special World War One Tribute Evening last year in aid of Poppyscotland, at which Club Members gave short speeches about "The Great War" in front of an invited audience.

Jim is a popular after-dinner speaker, particularly during the annual season of Burns Suppers, and he delights in giving talks on a variety of subjects to any group or society that invites him.

He has always been keen on poetry, winning the Glasgow Schools Scottish Recitation Competition at the age of 11 and writing his own verses since he was a boy. Many of his poems have been published over the years, the most recent being 'Kirriemuir' (q.v.) which won a place in United Press's 'Homeland collection' in 2013.

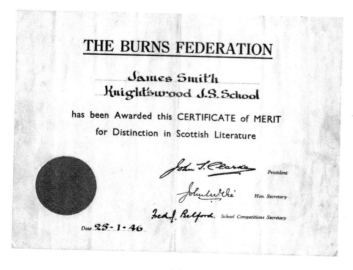

THE BURNS FEDERATION

James Smith
Knightswood J.S. School

has been Awarded this CERTIFICATE of MERIT
for Distinction in Scottish Literature

President

Hon. Secretary

School Competitions Secretary

Date 25-1-46